TEX-MEX
COOKING

GALLERY BOOKS

An Imprint of W. H. Smith Publishers Inc.
112 Madison Avenue
New York City 10016

INTRODUCTION

The Southwestern region of the United States is vast, with the landscape and climate varying from cool mountain ranges to hot, dry deserts and sun-drenched Gulf beaches. But for all its vastness and diversity, the regional recipes show a remarkable sense of unity.

The traditional ingredients of Tex-Mex cooking – chilies, corn, dried beans and squash – appear again and again. The traditional influences of Tex-Mex cooking – Indian and Hispanic – are evident, too, their stamp recognizable on many recipes still favored today.

Tortillas, either cornmeal or flour, are important as a base for toppings and sauces or as a substitute for bread rolls. Salsas, refried beans and chili, that well-known meat stew, are all part of Southwestern and Mexican cooking alike. This is Tex-Mex style, which most often symbolizes the food of the Southwest. There is more to it than that, though. Brook trout from mountain streams and seafood from the Gulf have their places, too, as do apricots and blueberries that grow so well here. There is also hearty ranch fare like barbecue ribs and pork stew.

As elsewhere, new influences are at work making food lighter and prettier, but the ingredients that have been traditional in the region for generations still prevail, making the food recognizably Tex-Mex no matter how the style changes.

MAKES 2 cups

RED PEPPER PRESERVES

This sweet but hot and spicy condiment adds
a bright spot of color and Tex-Mex
flavor to a main course or appetizer.

5 red peppers, seeded
3 red or green chilies, seeded
1½ cups sugar
¾ cup red wine vinegar
1 cup liquid pectin

2. Combine the sugar and vinegar in a deep, heavy-based pan and heat gently to dissolve the sugar.

3. Add the peppers and bring the mixture to the boil. Simmer for about 15 or 20 minutes.

4. Stir in the pectin and return the mixture to the boil over high heat.

5. Pour into sterilized jars and seal. Keep for up to one year in a cool, dark place.

Step 3 Add the chopped peppers and bring the mixture to the boil.

1. Chop the peppers and chilies finely in a food processor.

Step 4 Stir in the pectin and return the mixture to the boil.

Cook's Notes

Preparation
To sterilize the storage jars, place them in boiling water and boil for 15 minutes. Drain the jars upside down on paper towels and then fill them with the hot preserves to within about ½ inch of the top. Pour a layer of melted wax directly on top of the preserves to seal. When preserves have cooled and the wax has solidified, cover the jars with their lids. Waxed paper discs may also be used. If desired, the sealing process may be omitted and the preserves stored tightly covered in the refrigerator. Refrigerator-stored preserves will not keep as long.

Time
Preparation takes about 20 minutes and cooking takes about 20-25 minutes.

Serving Ideas
Serve as a condiment with meat, poultry, vegetable, egg or cheese dishes.

MAKES 4 cups

HOT PEPPER RELISH

Prepare this colorful relish in the summer,
when peppers are plentiful, but save some
to brighten up winter meals, too.

3lbs sweet peppers (even numbers of red, green, yellow
   and orange, or as available), seeded
4-6 red or green chilies, seeded and finely chopped
2 medium onions, finely chopped
½ tsp oregano
½ tsp ground coriander
2 bay leaves
Salt to taste
2 cups granulated or preserving sugar
1½ cups white wine vinegar or white distilled vinegar

Step 4 Drain the peppers and add them to the vinegar and sugar with the remaining ingredients.

Step 4 Spoon or ladle into sterilized preserving jars.

Step 2 Place the diced peppers and chilies in a large saucepan and pour over enough water to barely cover.

1. Cut the peppers into small dice and combine with the chilies and onions in a large saucepan.

2. Pour over boiling water to cover, and return to the boil. Cook rapidly for 10 minutes and drain well.

3. Meanwhile, combine the sugar and vinegar in a large saucepan. Bring slowly to the boil to dissolve the sugar, stirring occasionally.

4. When the peppers and onions have drained, add them and the remaining ingredients to the vinegar and sugar. Bring back to the boil and then simmer for 30 minutes. Remove the bay leaves and pour into sterilized jars and seal.

Cook's Notes

Time
Preparation takes about 30 minutes and cooking takes about 45 minutes.

Preparation
Sterilize the jars for storage in the same way as for Red Pepper Preserves. Omit the covering of wax, and seal the jars immediately. Store in a cool, dark place for up to one year, or cover tightly and keep in the refrigerator for a shorter time.

Serving Ideas
Serve as a condiment with cheese, egg and meat dishes. Relish is also good served with fish or shellfish.

MAKES 10

TORTILLAS

Borrowed from Mexico, these have become
indispensible in Tex-Mex cooking and
are used in a variety of delicious ways.

2 cups all-purpose flour (more if necessary)
2 tsps baking powder
Pinch salt
4 tbsps vegetable shortening
½-¾ cup hot water
Oil for frying

Step 1 After water
is added, knead
the dough gently,
adding more flour
if it is too sticky.

1. Sift the flour, baking powder and salt into a bowl. Rub in the vegetable shortening until the mixture resembles coarse crumbs. Add water, mixing until absorbed. Knead gently and add more flour if the dough is too sticky. Cover and leave to rest for 15 minutes.

2. Divide the dough into ten even-sized pieces. Roll into balls on a floured surface, cover and leave to stand for 20 minutes.

3. Roll out each ball on a lightly floured surface to a circle

7 inches in diameter. Cover the finished tortillas while rolling all the remaining dough.

4. Place a lightly oiled frying pan over high heat. Fry the tortillas individually on both sides until bubbles form on the surface. Stack them as they are cooked and set them aside until ready to use.

Step 3 Roll out
even-sized balls of
dough into circles
on a lightly-floured
surface.

Step 4 Fry the
tortillas in a lightly-
oiled frying pan
until bubbles
appear on the
surface.

Cook's Notes

 Time
Preparation takes about 50 minutes, including 35 minutes for the dough to rest. Cooking takes about 3 minutes per tortilla.

 Freezing
Stack the tortillas between sheets of plastic wrap or wax paper and place in freezer bags. Freeze for up to 6 months and defrost at room temperature. Use as indicated in the recipe. Tortillas may also be prepared in advance and kept in the refrigerator for several days.

Serving Ideas
Tortillas are used as a base for tacos, enchiladas and other Mexican or Tex-Mex dishes. They may also be served warm as an accompaniment to a main course. If desired, cut into triangles and deep-fry to serve with dips.

SERVES 4

CORNMEAL PANCAKES

Cornmeal, either yellow, white or blue, is an important
ingredient in Tex-Mex recipes. Here it's combined
with corn in a light and different kind of appetizer.

1 cup yellow cornmeal
1 tbsp flour
1 tsp baking soda
1 tsp salt
2 cups buttermilk
2 eggs, separated
Oil
10oz frozen corn
Red pepper preserves
Green onions, chopped
Sour cream

1. Sift the dry ingredients into a bowl, adding any coarse meal that remains in the strainer.

2. Mix the egg yolks and buttermilk together and gradually beat into the dry ingredients. Cover and leave to stand for at least 15 minutes.

3. Whisk the egg whites until stiff but not dry and fold into the cornmeal mixture.

4. Lightly grease a frying pan with oil and drop in about 2 tbsps of batter. Sprinkle with the corn and allow to cook until the underside is golden brown. Turn the pancakes and cook the second side until golden. Continue with the remaining batter and corn. Keep the cooked pancakes warm.

5. To serve, place three pancakes on warm side plates. Add a spoonful of sour cream and red pepper preserves to each and sprinkle over finely sliced or shredded green onions.

Step 2 Mix the egg yolks and buttermilk and gradually beat into the dry ingredients. Mixture will thicken on standing.

Step 3 Fold in stiffly-beaten egg whites with a large metal spoon or rubber spatula.

Step 4 Sprinkle the uncooked sides of the pancakes with some of the corn before turning over to cook further.

Cook's Notes

Time
Preparation takes about 30 minutes, including standing time for the pancake batter. Cooking takes about 3-4 minutes per pancake.

Cook's Tip
Allowing the pancake batter to stand 15 minutes before using it will produce a batter that is lighter and easier to use. This standing time also helps the cornmeal to soften.

Serving Ideas
Serve as an appetizer with the Red Pepper Preserves, sour cream and green onions or serve alone as a side dish to a main course.

SERVES 2

DENVER OMELET

This is a quick and easy meal for busy people
or unexpected company. If prepared like scrambled
eggs, the mixture can double as a sandwich filling.

4 strips bacon, diced
Half a small onion, chopped
Half a small green pepper, seeded and chopped
1 tomato, seeded and diced
3 eggs, beaten
Salt and pepper
1 tbsp grated cheese
Dash tabasco (optional)
Chopped parsley to garnish

Step 3 Pour in the egg, tomato and cheese mixture and stir once or twice to mix thoroughly.

Step 2 Cook the onion, green pepper and bacon until the vegetables are soft and the bacon is crisp.

Step 4 Place under a pre-heated broiler to cook the top until golden brown and slightly puffy.

1. Heat a medium-size frying pan or omelet pan. Add the bacon and sauté slowly until the fat is rendered.

2. Turn up the heat and cook until the bacon begins to brown and crisp. Add the onion and green pepper and cook to soften and finish off the bacon.

3. Mix the tomato with the eggs, salt, pepper, cheese and tabasco, if using. Pour into the pan and stir once or twice

with a fork to mix all the ingredients. Cook until lightly browned on the underside.

4. Place under a pre-heated broiler and cook the top quickly until brown and slightly puffy.

5. Sprinkle with parsley, cut into wedges and serve immediately.

 Cook's Notes

 Time
Preparation takes about 25 minutes and cooking takes about 10-15 minutes.

Cook's Tip
1 tbsp of water added to the eggs before beating will produce a lighter, fluffier omelet.

Serving Ideas
Serve as a light main course for supper or lunch. As an appetizer, this will serve 4 people.

SERVES 6

CHICKEN NUEVA MEXICANA

6 chicken thighs, skinned and boned
2 tbsps mild chili powder
2 tbsps oil
Juice of 1 lime
Pinch salt

Lime Cream Sauce

¾ cup sour cream or natural yogurt
1 tsp lime juice and grated rind
6 tbsps heavy cream
Salt

Corn Crêpes

1 cup fine yellow cornmeal
½ cup flour
Pinch salt
1 whole egg and 1 egg yolk
1 tbsp oil or melted butter or margarine
1½ cups milk

Garden Salsa

1 large zucchini
1 large ripe tomato
2 shallots
1 tbsp chopped fresh coriander
Pinch cayenne, pepper and salt
1 tbsp white wine vinegar
3 tbsps oil

Avocado and Orange Salad

2 oranges
1 avocado, peeled and sliced
Juice of 1 lime
Pinch sugar
Pinch coriander
6 tbsps pine nuts, toasted

1. Place the chicken in a shallow dish.
2. Combine the chili powder, oil, lime juice and salt and pour over the chicken. Turn the pieces over and rub the marinade into all the surfaces. Cover and refrigerate for 2 hours.
3. Combine all the ingredients for the Lime Cream Sauce and fold together gently. Cover and leave 2 hours in the refrigerator to thicken.

4. Sift the cornmeal, flour and salt for the crêpes into a bowl or a food processor. Combine the eggs, oil and milk. Make a well in the center of the ingredients in the bowl and pour in the liquid.
5. Stir the liquid ingredients with a wooden spoon to gradually incorporate the dry ingredients. Alternatively, combine all the ingredients in a food processor and process until smooth. Leave the batter to stand for 30 minutes whichever method you choose.
6. Trim the ends of zucchini and cut into small dice. Peel the tomatoes and remove the seeds. Cut the tomato flesh into small dice. Cut the shallots into dice the same size as the zucchini and tomato.
7. Combine the coriander, cayenne pepper, vinegar, oil and salt, mixing very well. Pour over the vegetables and stir to mix. Cover and leave to marinate.
8. Heat a small amount of oil in a large frying pan and place in the chicken in a single layer. Fry quickly to brown both sides. Pour over remaining marinade, cover and cook until tender, about 25 minutes.
9. Heat a small amount of oil in an 8 inch crêpe or frying pan. Wipe out with paper towel and return the pan to the heat until hot.
10. Pour a spoonful of the batter into the pan and swirl to coat the bottom with the mixture. Make sure the edge of each crêpe is irregular.
11. When the edges of each crêpe look pale brown and the top surface begins to bubble, turn the crêpes using a palette knife. Cook the other side. Stack as each is finished Cover with foil and keep warm in a low oven.
12. Pour about 2 tbsps oil into a small frying pan and when hot add the pine nuts. Cook over moderate heat, stirring constantly until golden brown. Remove and drain on paper towels.
13. Peel and segment the oranges over a bowl to catch the juice. Cut the avocado in half, remove the stone and peel. Cut into thin slices and combine with the orange. Add the remaining ingredients for the salad, except the pine nuts, and toss gently to mix.
14. To assemble, place one corn crêpe on a serving plate. Place one piece of chicken on the lower half of the crêpe, top with a spoonful of Lime Cream Sauce. Place a serving of Garden Salsa and one of Avocado and Orange Salad on either side of the chicken and partially fold the crêpe over the top. Scatter over pine nuts and serve immediately.

Cook's Notes

Preparation
Because the dish is complicated, several of its many parts may be prepared well in advance. The chicken may be marinated longer than 2 hours in the refrigerator, overnight if desired. The Lime Cream Sauce can remain in the refrigerator overnight and so can the Garden Salsa. The Corn Crêpes can be prepared in advance and kept covered in the refrigerator. They may also be frozen with sheets of wax paper in between. Defrost at room temperature and then re-heat.

SERVES 4

CHICKEN WITH RED PEPPERS

Easy as this recipe is, it looks and tastes good
enough for guests. The warm taste of roasted
red peppers is typically Tex-Mex.

4 large red peppers
4 skinned and boned chicken breasts
1½ tbsps oil
Salt and pepper
1 clove garlic, finely chopped
3 tbsps white wine vinegar
2 green onions, finely chopped
Sage leaves for garnish

Step 1 Flatten the peppers with the palm of the hand and brush them with oil.

1. Cut the peppers in half and remove the stems, cores and seeds. Flatten the peppers with the palm of your hand and brush the skin sides lightly with oil.

2. Place the peppers skin side up on the rack of a pre-heated broiler and cook about 2 inches away from the heat source until the skins are well blistered and charred.

3. Wrap the peppers in a clean towel and allow them to stand until cool. Peel off the skins with a small vegetable knife. Cut into thin strips and set aside.

4. Place the chicken breasts between two sheets of plastic wrap and flatten by hitting with a rolling pin or meat mallet.

5. Heat 1½ tbsps oil in a large frying pan. Season the

chicken breasts on both sides and place in the hot oil. Cook 5 minutes, turn over and cook until tender and lightly browned. Remove the chicken and keep it warm.

6. Add the pepper strips, garlic, vinegar and green onions to the pan and cook briefly until the vinegar loses its strong aroma.

7. Slice the chicken breasts across the grain into ¼ inch thick slices and arrange on serving plates. Spoon over the pan juices.

8. Arrange the pepper mixture with the chicken and garnish with the sage leaves.

Step 2 Cook the peppers until the skins are blistered and well charred.

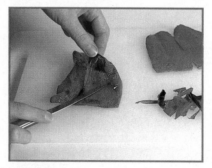

Step 3 Peel off the skins using a small vegetable knife.

Cook's Notes

Time
Preparation takes about 35-40 minutes and cooking takes about 10 minutes to char the peppers and about 20 minutes to finish the dish.

Variation
For convenience, the dish may be prepared with canned pimento caps instead of red peppers. These will be softer so cook the garlic, vinegar and onions to soften, and then add pimento.

Buying Guide
Sage is a very common herb in the Southwestern United States. If unavailable fresh, substitute coriander or parsley leaves as a garnish.

SERVES 4

SOUTHWESTERN STIR-FRY

East meets West in a dish that is lightning-
fast to cook. Baby corn, traditionally
Oriental, echoes the Southwestern love of corn.

1lb sirloin or rump steak
2 cloves garlic, crushed
6 tbsps wine vinegar
6 tbsps oil
Pinch sugar, salt and pepper
1 bay leaf
1 tbsp ground cumin
1 small red pepper, seeded and sliced
1 small green pepper, seeded and sliced
2oz baby corn
4 green onions, shredded
Oil for frying

Red Sauce

8 fresh ripe tomatoes, peeled, seeded and chopped
4 tbsps oil
1 medium onion, finely chopped
1-2 green chilies, finely chopped
1-2 cloves garlic, crushed
6 sprigs fresh coriander
3 tbsps tomato paste

Step 1 Slice the meat thinly across the grain.

1. Slice the meat thinly across the grain. Combine in a plastic bag with the next 6 ingredients. Tie the bag and toss the ingredients inside to coat. Place in a bowl and leave about 4 hours.

2. Heat the oil for the sauce and cook the onion, chilies and garlic to soften but not brown. Add remaining sauce ingredients and cook about 15 minutes over gentle heat. Purée in a food processor until smooth.

3. Heat a frying pan and add the meat in three batches, discarding the marinade. Cook to brown and set aside. Add about 2 tbsps of oil and cook the peppers about 2 minutes. Add the corn and onions and return the meat to the pan. Cook a further 1 minute and add the sauce. Cook to heat through and serve immediately.

Step 3 Cook the meat quickly over high heat to brown.

Step 3 Add the remaining ingredients and enough sauce to coat all ingredients thoroughly.

Cook's Notes

Time
Preparation takes about 25 minutes, with 4 hours for marinating the meat. The sauce takes about 15 minutes to cook and the remaining ingredients need about 6-7 minutes.

Preparation
The sauce may be prepared ahead of time and kept in the refrigerator for several days. It may also be frozen. Defrost the sauce at room temperature and then boil rapidly to reduce it again slightly.

Buying Guide
Baby corn is available from greengrocers and supermarkets. It is also available canned in delicatessens and supermarkets that stock Oriental cooking ingredients.

SERVES 6-8

CHILI ROJA

Red meat, red onions, red peppers, paprika,
tomatoes and red beans all give clues to
the name of this zesty stew.

2lbs beef chuck, cut into 1 inch pieces
Oil
1 large red onion, coarsely chopped
2 cloves garlic, crushed
2 red peppers, seeded and cut into 1 inch pieces
1-2 red chilies, seeded and finely chopped
3 tbsps mild chili powder
1 tbsp cumin
1 tbsp paprika
3 cups beer, water or stock
8oz canned tomatoes, puréed
2 tbsps tomato paste
8oz canned red kidney beans, drained
Pinch salt
6 ripe tomatoes, peeled, seeded and diced

1. Pour about 4 tbsps oil into a large saucepan or flameproof casserole. When hot, brown the meat in small batches over moderately high heat for about 5 minutes per batch.

2. Set aside the meat on a plate or in the lid of the casserole. Lower the heat and cook the onion, garlic, red peppers and chilies for about 5 minutes. Add the chili powder, cumin and paprika and cook for 1 minute further. Pour on the liquid and add the canned tomatoes, tomato paste and the meat.

3. Cook slowly for about 1½-2 hours. Add the beans about 45 minutes before the end of cooking time.

4. When the meat is completely tender, add salt to taste and serve garnished with the diced tomatoes.

Step 2 Cook the onions, garlic, red peppers and chilies slowly until slightly softened.

Step 2 If using beer, add it very slowly as it will tend to foam up in the heat of the pan.

Cook's Notes

Time
Preparation takes about 25 minutes and cooking takes about 1½-2 hours.

Freezing
The chili may be frozen for up to 3 months in a tightly covered freezer container. Allow the chili to cool completely before sealing and freezing. Defrost in the refrigerator and bring slowly to the boil before serving.

Variation
The chili may be made with pork shoulder or with a mixture of beef and pork. Although not authentic, the chili may also be made with ground beef or pork.

SERVES 6

BARBECUED RIBS

No Tex-Mex cookbook would be complete
without a barbecue recipe. This versatile
sauce keeps well in the refrigerator, too.

4½lbs pork spare ribs
1 cup tomato ketchup
2 tsps mustard powder
4 tbsps Worcester sauce
2 tbsps vinegar
4 tbsps brown sugar
Half a chili, seeded and finely chopped
Half a small onion, finely chopped
4 tbsps water
Salt (if necessary)

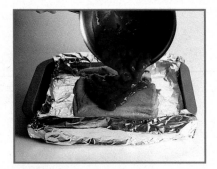

Step 3 Uncover
the ribs and pour
over the sauce.

Step 4 To serve,
cut the ribs into
individual pieces
between the
bones.

Step 1 Cook the
ribs in a roasting
pan at a high
temperature for 15
minutes.

1. Place the ribs in a roasting pan and cover with foil. Cook
for 15 minutes at 425°F.

2. Meanwhile, combine all the sauce ingredients in a
heavy-based pan and bring to the boil. Reduce heat and
simmer for about 15 minutes.

3. Reduce the oven temperature to 350°F and uncover

the ribs. Pour over the sauce and bake a further hour,
basting frequently.

4. Remove the ribs from the roasting pan and reserve the
sauce. Place the ribs on a cutting board and slice into
individual rib pieces, between the bones.

5. Skim any fat from the surface of the sauce and serve the
sauce separately.

Cook's Notes

Time
Preparation takes about 30
minutes and cooking takes
about 1 hour 15 minutes.

Variation
The sauce is also good served
on pork chops, chicken or
steaks.

Serving Ideas
Serve with Spicy Beans and
Rice or Refried Beans. Add
warm tortillas and a salad.

SERVES 4

BARBECUED PORK STEW

Named for the sauce rather than the
cooking method, this stew requires long,
slow cooking to bring out its flavor.

2lb pork shoulder, cut in 2 inch cubes
Oil
2 medium onions, cut in 2 inch pieces
1 large green pepper, seeded and cut in 2 inch pieces
1 tbsp chili powder
2 cloves garlic, crushed
1lb canned tomatoes
3 tbsps tomato paste
1 tbsp Worcester sauce
½ cup water or beef stock
2 tbsps cider vinegar
1 bay leaf
½ tsp dried oregano
Salt and a few drops tabasco sauce

Step 1 Brown the pork cubes in oil over high heat in a large frying pan.

Step 2 Combine the ingredients and stir well to break up the tomatoes slightly.

1. Heat about 2 tbsps oil in a large sauté or frying pan. When hot, add the pork cubes in two batches. Brown over high heat for about 5 minutes per batch. Remove to a plate. Add more oil if necessary and cook the onions and peppers to soften slightly. Add the chili powder and garlic and cook 1 minute more.

2. Add the tomatoes, their juice and the tomato paste. Stir in the Worcester sauce, water or stock and vinegar breaking up the tomatoes slightly. Add bay leaf, oregano and salt.

3. Transfer to a flameproof casserole dish. Bring the mixture to the boil and then cook slowly for about 1½ hours, covered.

4. When the meat is completely tender, skim any fat from the surface of the sauce, remove the bay leaf and add a few drops of tabasco sauce to taste. Adjust salt and serve.

Step 4 When the meat is tender, skim excess fat from the surface of the sauce with a spoon, or blot up with strips of paper towel.

Cook's Notes

Time
Preparation takes about 25 minutes and cooking takes about 1½ hours.

Freezing
Allow the stew to cool completely. Spoon into freezer containers, cover tightly and freeze for up to 3 months. Defrost in the refrigerator and then slowly bring to the boil to re-heat before serving.

Serving Ideas
Accompany with warm tortillas and serve Spicy Rice and Beans as a side dish.

SERVES 6-8

CHILI VERDE

A chili, really a spicy meat
stew, is as traditional in the
Southwest as it is in Mexico.

2lbs lean pork, cut into 1inch pieces
Oil
3 green peppers, seeded and cut into 1 inch pieces
1-2 green chili peppers, seeded and finely chopped
1 small bunch green onions, chopped
2 cloves garlic, crushed
2 tsps ground cumin
2 tsps chopped fresh oregano
3 tbsps chopped fresh coriander
1 bay leaf
3 cups beer, water or chicken stock
8oz canned chickpeas, drained
1½ tbsps cornstarch mixed with 3 tbsps cold water
   (optional)
Salt
1 large ripe avocado, peeled and diced
1 tbsp lime juice

1. Heat 4 tbsps of oil and lightly brown the pork cubes over high heat. Use a large flameproof casserole and brown the pork in 2 or 3 batches.

2. Lower the heat and cook the peppers to soften slightly. Add the chilies, onions, garlic and cumin and cook for 2 minutes.

3. Add the herbs and liquid and reduce the heat. Simmer, covered, 1-1½ hours or until the meat is tender. Add the chickpeas during the last 45 minutes.

4. If necessary, thicken with the cornstarch, stirring constantly after adding until the liquid thickens and clears.

5. Add salt to taste and remove the bay leaf.

6. Toss the avocado in lime juice and sprinkle over the top of the chili to serve.

Step 1 The pork should barely begin to take on color. Do not over brown.

Step 4 If necessary, add the cornstarch mixture to thicken, stirring constantly.

Cook's Notes

Time
Preparation takes about 30-40 minutes and cooking takes about 1-1½ hours.

Variation
Vary the amount of chili peppers, garlic and herbs to suit your own taste.

Serving Ideas
Serve for lunch or a light supper with warm tortillas.

SERVES 4

RIVERSIDE TROUT

Brook trout is so delicious that simple preparation
is all that's necessary. Crisp cornmeal, bacon and
pine nuts complement the fresh flavor.

⅓-½ cup vegetable oil
4 tbsps pine nuts
8 strips bacon, diced
1 cup yellow cornmeal
Pinch salt and white pepper
4 trout weighing about 8oz each, cleaned
Juice of 1 lime
Fresh sage or coriander

1. Heat 6 tbsps of the oil in a large frying pan. Add the pine nuts and cook over moderate heat, stirring constantly. When a pale golden brown, remove them with a draining spoon to paper towels.

2. Add the diced bacon to the oil and cook until crisp, stirring constantly. Drain with the pine nuts.

3. Mix the cornmeal, salt and pepper, and dredge the fish well, patting on the cornmeal. Shake off any excess.

4. If necessary, add more oil to the pan – it should come about halfway up the sides of the fish. Re-heat over moderately high heat.

5. When hot, add the fish two at a time and fry until golden brown, about 4-5 minutes. Turn over and reduce the heat slightly if necessary and cook a further 4-5 minutes. Drain and repeat with the remaining fish.

6. Drain almost all the oil from the pan and re-heat the bacon and the nuts very briefly. Add the lime juice and cook a few seconds. Spoon the bacon and pine nut mixture over the fish and garnish with coriander or sage.

Step 3 Dredge the fish with the cornmeal mixture, shaking off any excess.

Step 5 Place the fish two at a time in hot oil and fry until golden brown on one side, then turn.

Step 6 Spoon the bacon, pine nut and lime juice mixture over the fish.

 Cook's Notes

 **Time**
Preparation takes about 25 minutes and cooking takes about 15-20 minutes.

Preparation
When dredging fish, seafood or chicken with flour or cornmeal to coat, prepare just before ready to cook. If the food stands with its coating for too long before cooking, the coating will become soggy.

Variation
If desired, the trout may be dredged with plain or whole-wheat flour instead of the cornmeal.

SERVES 4

BROILED TROUT WITH PEPPER RELISH

Fresh trout, perfectly broiled, and spicy sweet pepper relish
make an unusual, innovative and very special dish.

1 lime
2 tbsps butter, melted
4 filleted trout, unskinned (double fillets preferred)
8 tbsps prepared hot pepper relish
Lime wedges or coriander leaves to garnish

Step 3 Place fillets on a broiler rack and baste with the butter and lime juice mixture.

1. Remove the rind of the lime with a citrus zester and set it aside.

2. Squeeze the juice and mix with the butter.

3. Place the fish fillets on a broiler rack and baste with the butter and lime juice mixture. Place under a pre-heated broiler for about 4-5 minutes, depending on the thickness of the fillets. Baste frequently.

4. Pour over any remaining butter and lime juice and sprinkle the fish with the lime zest.

5. Gently re-heat the relish and spoon 2 tbsps down the center of each of the double fillets. Garnish with lime or coriander.

Step 4 Sprinkle the fish with the lime zest.

Step 5 Spoon the pepper relish down the center of the double fillets.

Cook's Notes

Time
Preparation takes about 20 minutes if using pre-prepared pepper relish.

Buying Guide
Trout fillets are available from fishmongers and fish departments in supermarkets. Unskinned fillets hold their shape much better when cooked.

Watchpoint
When re-heating the pepper relish, watch it closely as it has a high quantity of sugar and can burn easily.

SERVES 4

FRIED BASS IN CORNMEAL

As a coating for frying, cornmeal is
superb. It fries to a crisp crunch and
adds a subtle flavor of its own.

2lb freshwater bass or other whitefish fillets
Milk
2 cups yellow cornmeal
2 tbsps flour
Pinch salt
2 tsps cayenne pepper
1 tsp ground cumin
2 tsps garlic granules
Lime wedges to garnish

Step 3 Mix the cornmeal coating on a sheet of wax paper, place on the fish and lift the ends to toss and coat.

Step 2 Dip the fillets into milk and then hold by one end to allow the excess to drip off.

Step 5 Turn the fish over once it floats to the surface of the oil.

1. Mix the cornmeal, flour, salt, cayenne, cumin and garlic together in a shallow container or on a piece of wax paper.

2. Skin the fillets if desired. Dip them into the milk and then lift to allow the excess to drip off.

3. Place the fish in the cornmeal mixture and turn with two forks or, if using paper, lift the ends and toss the fish to coat.

4. Meanwhile, heat oil in a deep frying pan, large saucepan or deep fat fryer.

5. Add the fish in small batches and cook until the fillets float to the surface. Turn over and cook to brown lightly and evenly.

6. Drain on paper towels and serve immediately with lime wedges.

Cook's Notes

Time
Preparation takes about 20 minutes and cooking takes about 5 minutes per batch of fish.

Serving Ideas
Red pepper preserves or hot pepper relish may be served as a condiment with this fish, or accompany it with either the Garden Salsa or the Orange and Avocado Salad from the Chicken Nueva Mexicana recipe.

Variation
If substituting another type of fish for bass, make sure that it is a firm-fleshed fish.

SERVES 4

SWORDFISH WITH GRAPEFRUIT TEQUILA SALSA

Rich and dense in texture, swordfish takes very well to
a tart grapefruit accompaniment with a dash of tequila.

4-6 ruby or pink grapefruit (depending on size)
1 lime
Half a green chili, seeded and finely diced
1 green onion, finely chopped
2 tbsps chopped fresh coriander
1 tbsp sugar
3 tbsps tequila
4-8 swordfish steaks (depending on size)
Juice of 1 lime
2 tbsps oil
Black pepper to taste
Coriander sprigs for garnish

1. Remove the zest from the grapefruit and lime with a zester and set it aside.

2. Remove all the pith from the grapefruit and segment them. Squeeze the lime for juice. Mix the grapefruit and citrus zests with the chilli, onion, coriander, sugar, tequila and lime juice and set aside.

3. Mix remaining lime juice, oil and pepper together and brush both sides of the fish. Place under a pre-heated broiler and cook for about 4 minutes each side depending on distance from the heat source.

4. To serve, place a coriander sprig on each fish steak and serve with the grapefruit salsa.

Step 1 Remove the zest from the grapefruit with a zester.

Step 2 Use a serrated fruit knife to remove all the pith from the grapefruit.

Cook's Notes

Time
Preparation takes about 35 minutes and cooking takes about 4-6 minutes.

Variation
If desired, substitute white rum for the tequila in the salsa or omit it altogether. The amount of sugar needed will vary depending on the sweetness of the grapefruit.

Cook's Tip
For extra flavor, the swordfish steaks may be marinated in a lime juice and oil mixture for up to 1 hour.

SERVES 6

GULF COAST TACOS

Around the Gulf of Mexico, ever
popular tacos take on a new look
and taste with a seafood filling.

6 Tortillas (see recipe)

Green Chili Salsa

3 tomatillos, husks removed
1 tbsp oil
1 clove garlic
1oz coriander
2 green chilies
Juice of 1 lime
Pinch salt and sugar
½ cup sour cream

Filling Ingredients

8oz large raw shrimp, peeled
8oz raw scallops, quartered if large
1 tsp coriander seed, crushed
1 shallot, finely chopped
Salt and pepper
6 tbsps white wine
Water
1 small jicama, peeled and cut into thin matchstick strips
Coriander leaves and lime wedges

1. Prepare the Tortillas according to the recipe.

2. Heat 1 tbsp of oil in a small frying pan and slice the tomatillos. Sauté them for about 3 minutes to soften. Place in a food processor along with the garlic, coriander, chilies and lime juice. Purée until smooth. Fold in the sour cream, adjust seasoning and chill.

3. Heat oil in a deep sauté pan to a depth of at least 2 inches. When hot, place in a tortilla and press down under the oil with a metal spoon. When the tortilla starts to puff up, take it out and immediately fold to form a shell. Hold in shape until it cools slightly and sets. Repeat with the remaining tortillas. Keep them warm in an oven, standing on their open ends.

4. Place the shrimp, scallops, coriander seeds, shallot and salt and pepper in a sauté pan with the wine and water to barely cover. Cook for about 8 minutes, stirring occasionally. The shrimp should turn pink and the scallops will look opaque when cooked.

5. Fill the taco shells with the jicama. Remove the seafood from the liquid with a draining spoon and arrange on top of the jicama. Top with the salsa and decorate with coriander leaves. Serve with lime wedges.

Step 3 Carefully fold over the tortilla to form a shell and hold in shape until it cools slightly and sets.

Step 4 Cook filling ingredients for eight minutes, until the shrimp turn pink and the scallops look opaque when cooked.

Cook's Notes

Time
Preparation takes about 1 hour, including the time to make the tortillas.

Variation
If desired, this recipe may be made with pre-prepared tortillas or taco shells. If using taco shells, simply re-heat in the oven, standing on their open ends.

Cook's Tip
Heating taco shells standing on their open ends keeps them from closing up.

SERVES 4

CHEESE OR VEGETABLE ENCHILADAS

Many dishes in Tex-Mex cooking have Mexican
origins, like these tortillas filled with a choice of fillings.

8 Tortillas (see recipe)
Full quantity Red Sauce (see Southwestern Stir-fry)

Cheese Filling

2 tbsps oil
1 small red pepper, seeded and finely diced
1 clove garlic, crushed
1 tbsp chopped fresh coriander
½ cup heavy cream
½ cup cream cheese
½ cup mild cheese, grated
Whole coriander leaves

Vegetable Filling

2 tbsps oil
1 small onion, finely chopped
1 green pepper, seeded and diced
2 zucchini, diced
½ tsp oregano
½ tsp ground cumin
4oz corn, fresh or frozen
Salt and pepper
1½ cups grated mild cheese
Sour cream
Full quantity green chili salsa (see Gulf Coast Tacos)

1. Prepare the tortillas, red sauce and green chili salsa according to the recipe directions.

2. Heat the oil for the cheese filling and cook the pepper and garlic slowly to soften. Add the coriander and pour in the cream.

3. Bring to the boil and cook rapidly to thicken. Add the cream cheese and stir to melt. Add the grated mild cheese, stir in and keep the filling warm.

4. Re-heat the tortillas wrapped in foil in a moderate oven for about 10 minutes. Place one at a time on serving dishes

and spoon in the cheese filling. Fold over both sides to the middle.

5. Re-heat the red sauce, if necessary, and spoon over the center of two enchiladas. Garnish with coriander leaves.

6. For the vegetable filling, heat the oil and cook the onion to soften. Add the remaining vegetables except the corn. Add the oregano and cumin and cook about 3 minutes or until the onions are soft. Add the corn and heat through, adding seasoning to taste. Stir in the grated cheese and fill the tortillas as before, but place in a baking dish. Cook, covered, for about 10-15 minutes at 350°F, or until the cheese has melted and the filling is beginning to bubble. Serve topped with sour cream and green chili salsa.

Step 5 Place two tortillas on a serving plate and spoon over the red sauce.

Step 6 Place tortilla at one end of the baking dish, spoon in the filling and fold over. Repeat with the remaining tortillas and filling.

Cook's Notes

Time
Preparation takes about 1 hour. Cheese filling takes about 10 minutes to cook and the vegetable filling takes 13-18 minutes.

Serving Ideas
Serve with Refried Beans or Spicy Rice and Beans. Add green salad or sliced avocado.

MAKES 10

CHALUPAS

These are tortillas in another form, this time a snack
with spicy meat. Create your own combination
with a selection of different toppings.

Half quantity Tortilla recipe
Oil for frying
Full quantity Red Sauce (see recipe for Southwestern Stir-
fry)
12oz ground beef
2 cloves garlic, crushed
1 tsp dried oregano
2 tsps cumin
Salt and pepper
3oz frozen corn
4 tbsps raisins

Toppings

6-8 chopped green onions
4-6 diced tomatoes
Half a small head lettuce, shredded
½ cup sour cream
1 cup shredded cheese

1. Prepare the tortillas according to the recipe and divide
the dough in 10. After the required resting time, roll the balls
of dough into 3½ inch rounds.

2. Prepare the Red Sauce according to the recipe
instructions and set it aside.

3. Heat at least 2 inches of oil in a frying pan, sauté pan or
medium saucepan. When hot, place in one tortilla and fry
briefly until just crisp. Drain and keep them warm.

4. Cook the beef slowly until the fat begins to render. Add
the garlic, oregano and cumin and raise the heat to brown
the meat. Season to taste and then stir in enough of the Red
Sauce to moisten the meat well. Add the corn and raisins,
cover the pan and leave to stand for 5 minutes.

5. Spoon the meat onto the tortillas and drizzle over more
sauce. Garnish with your choice of toppings.

Step 4 Add
enough of the
sauce to moisten
the meat thoroughly.

Step 5 Spoon the
meat onto the
tortillas and add
more sauce and
topping.

Cook's Notes

Time
Preparation takes about 40
minutes and cooking takes
about 30 seconds for the tortillas, 15
minutes for the sauce and about 15
minutes to finish the beef topping.

Variation
Refried Beans may be used
instead of the beef topping, if
desired. About half quantity of the
Refried Bean recipe should be enough
to top 10 Chalupas. Omit the corn and
raisins and use half quantity of the Red
Sauce recipe as a topping.

Serving Ideas
Serve as a snack or cocktail
savory. For a main course,
add Refried Beans or Spicy Rice and
Beans as an accompaniment.

SERVES 4-6

INDIAN BREAD WITH CHORIZO AND SALSA

A version of this bread recipe has been baked by American Indians
for hundreds of years. It's delicious served plain, too.

Bread

2 cups all-purpose flour
1 tbsp baking powder
Pinch salt
1 tbsp vegetable shortening
2 tsps cumin seed
¾ cup plus 2 tbsps water

Chorizo Topping

1lb chorizo sausage
2 medium red potatoes, scrubbed
4 green onions, chopped

Salsa

1 clove garlic
1oz coriander leaves
1 tsp fresh oregano
Half or less fresh red or green chili, seeded
Pinch salt and dry mustard
Juice of 2 limes
¾ cup oil
Shredded lettuce, crumbled goat's milk cheese and
    chopped tomatoes to garnish

1. Sift the flour, baking powder and salt into a bowl. Rub in the shortening until the mixture resembles coarse crumbs and then stir in the cumin seed. Stir in enough water to make a soft, slightly sticky dough. Knead several times. cover and leave to stand for 15-20 minutes.

2. Divide the dough into 8 pieces and roll or pat into 5 inch circles on a well-floured surface. Make a hole in the center of each with your finger and leave the circles to stand, covered, for 30 minutes.

3. Meanwhile, boil the potatoes in their skins in a covered saucepan. Place the chorizo in a sauté pan and cover with water. Cover the pan and bring to the boil. Lower the heat and simmer about 10 minutes, or until just tender. Remove the chorizo from the water and peel off the casings while the sausage is still warm. Chop sausage roughly and set aside. When the potatoes are tender, drain them and leave to cool. Cut the potatoes into ½ inch dice.

4. Place the garlic, coriander, oregano, chili, salt and mustard into a food processor and add the lime juice. Process until well blended. With the machine running, pour the oil through the funnel in a thin, steady stream. Process until smooth and adjust the seasoning.

5. Pour the oil for cooking the bread into a deep-fat fryer, large saucepan or deep sauté pan to a depth of about 2-3 inches. Heat to 375°F. Carefully lower in one dough circle and push it underneath the oil with a large metal spoon. Fry for about 30 seconds, turn over and fry the other side. Drain each while frying the others.

6. Mix the chorizo, green onions and potatoes with enough of the salsa to moisten. Arrange the shredded lettuce on top of the bread and spoon on the chorizo topping. Spoon on any remaining salsa, sprinkle with chopped tomato and crumbled cheese.

Cook's Notes

Time
Preparation takes about 45 minutes – 1 hour. Indian Bread will take about 1-2 minutes to cook per piece. The chorizo topping will take about 25 minutes for the potatoes and sausage to cook.

Preparation
Indian Bread is best prepared, cooked and eaten on the same day. If desired, the chorizo topping and salsa may be prepared in advance and kept in the refrigerator overnight. The salsa will keep 3-4 days, but may separate slightly during storage. Simply re-process or beat vigorously to bring the mixture back together.

Serving Ideas
The recipe directions are for serving the dish at room temperature. For serving hot, re-heat the chorizo topping and combine with the salsa. Place directly on the hot bread, saving the lettuce to garnish the top along with the tomatoes and cheese.

MAKES 12-14

CHURROS

These fritters can be either sweet
or savory. Either way, they're a
treat with a Mexican influence.

Basic Dough

Scant 1 cup plus 2 tbsps water
3 tbsps butter or margarine
Pinch salt
1 cup all-purpose flour
6 tbsps cornmeal
2 eggs
Oil for deep frying

Savory Ingredients

2 tbsps finely grated cheese
2 chili peppers, seeded and finely chopped
Parmesan cheese (optional)

Sweet Ingredients

4 tbsps sugar
1 tbsp unsweetened cocoa powder
1 tsp ground cinnamon
Powdered sugar (optional)

1. Combine the water, butter or margarine and salt in a heavy-based saucepan. If making sweet churros, add sugar as well. Cook over medium heat until the butter or margarine melts.

2. Immediately stir in the flour and cornmeal. Keeping the pan over medium heat, stir until the mixture pulls away from the sides of the pan and forms a ball. Take off the heat and cool slightly.

3. Add the eggs one at a time, beating vigorously in between each addition. It may not be necessary to add all the egg. Beat until the mixture is smooth and shiny and thick enough to pipe. Add the cheese and chilies *or* the cocoa and cinnamon with the eggs.

4. Spoon the mixture into a pastry bag fitted with a star tip.

5. Heat the oil in a deep fat fryer, deep saucepan or deep sauté pan to a depth of at least 4 inches. Pipe the dough into the oil in 10 inch strips and fry until golden brown, about 3 minutes per side. Drain on paper towels and sprinkle the savory churros with Parmesan cheese and the sweet with powdered sugar, if desired. Serve warm.

Step 2 Cook the mixture over moderate heat, stirring until it pulls away from the sides and forms a ball.

Step 5 Pipe the dough into the hot oil in long strips. They will curl and change shape as they cook.

Cook's Notes

Time
Preparation takes about 25-30 minutes and cooking takes about 6 minutes per piece.

Preparation
As the churros cook in the hot fat, they will curl into different shapes.

Cook's Tip
The mixture will be easier to pipe if it is used just after preparation.

SERVES 6-8

SPICY RICE AND BEANS

A lively side dish or vegetarian main course,
this recipe readily takes to creative variations
and even makes a good cold salad.

4 tbsps oil
2 cups long grain rice
1 onion, finely chopped
1 green pepper, seeded and chopped
1 tsp each ground cumin and coriander
1-2 tsps tabasco sauce
Salt
3½ cups stock
1lb canned red kidney beans, drained and rinsed
1lb canned tomatoes, drained and coarsely chopped
Chopped parsley

Step 2 Cook the rice in the oil until just turning opaque.

1. Heat the oil in a casserole or a large, deep saucepan.

2. Add the rice and cook until just turning opaque. Add the onion, pepper and cumin and coriander. Cook gently for a further 2 minutes.

3. Add the tabasco, salt, stock and beans and bring to the boil. Cover and cook about 45 minutes, or until the rice is tender and most of the liquid is absorbed.

4. Remove from the heat and add the tomatoes, stirring them in gently. Leave to stand, covered, for 5 minutes.

5. Fluff up the mixture with a fork and sprinkle with parsley to serve.

Step 3 Cook with the remaining ingredients until rice is tender and most of the liquid is absorbed.

Step 4 Carefully stir in the tomatoes before covering and leaving to stand.

Cook's Notes

 Time
Preparation takes about 25 minutes and cooking takes about 50 minutes.

Serving Ideas
Serve with warm tortillas and a salad for a light vegetarian meal. Serve as a side dish with enchiladas, meat or poultry, or cheese and egg dishes.

Variation
The recipe may be made with 1lb fresh tomatoes, peeled, seeded and coarsely chopped.

SERVES 6-8

REFRIED BEANS

This is a classic accompaniment to both
Mexican and Tex-Mex main courses be
they poultry or meat, vegetable or cheese.

8oz dried pinto beans
Water to cover
1 bay leaf
6 tbsps oil
Salt and pepper
Grated mild cheese
Shredded lettuce
Tortillas

Step 3 Turn the beans over when the bottom is set but not brown.

Step 2 As the beans fry in the oil, mash them with the back of a spoon.

Step 4 Sprinkle on the cheese and cook until it melts.

1. Soak the beans overnight. Change the water, add the bay leaf and bring to the boil. Cover and simmer about 2 hours, or until the beans are completely tender. Alternatively, bring the beans to the boil in cold water and then allow to boil rapidly for 10 minutes. Cover and leave to stand for one hour. Change the water and then continue with the recipe. Drain the beans and reserve a small amount of the cooking liquid. Discard bay leaf.

2. Heat the oil in a heavy frying pan. Add the beans and, as they fry, mash them with the back of a spoon. Do not over-

mash – about a third of the beans should stay whole. Season to taste.

3. Smooth out the beans in the pan and cook until the bottom is set but not browned. Turn the beans over and cook the other side.

4. Top with the cheese and cook the beans until the cheese melts. Serve with finely shredded lettuce and tortillas, either warm or cut in triangles and deep-fried until crisp.

Cook's Notes

Time
Preparation takes about 15 minutes. The beans must be soaked overnight or re-hydrated by the quick method. The beans must be cooked at least 2 hours before frying.

Watchpoint
Make sure the beans are completely tender and have boiled rapidly for at least 45 minutes before eating.

Serving Ideas
Serve the beans as a side dish with enchiladas or with barbecued meats.

SERVES 8

CHILI RELLENOS

Organization is the key to preparing these
stuffed peppers. Fried inside their golden
batter coating, they're puffy and light.

Full quantity Red Sauce (see recipe for Southwestern Stir-
fry)
8 small green peppers
4 small green chilies, seeded and finely chopped
1 clove garlic, crushed
1 tsp chopped fresh sage
8oz cream cheese
2 cups grated mild cheese
Salt
Flour for dredging
Oil for deep frying
8 eggs, separated
6 tbsps all-purpose flour
Pinch salt
Finely chopped green onions

1. Blanch the whole peppers in boiling water for about
10-15 minutes, or until just tender. Rinse them in cold water
and pat them dry.

2. Carefully cut around the stems to make a top, remove
and set aside. Scoop out the seeds and cores, leaving the
peppers whole. Leave upside down on paper towels to
drain.

3. Mix together the chilies, garlic, sage, cheeses and salt to
taste. Fill the peppers using a small teaspoon and replace
the tops, sticking them into the filling.

4. Dredge the peppers with flour and heat the oil in a deep
fat fryer to 375°F.

5. Beat the egg yolks and flour in a mixing bowl until the
mixture forms a ribbon trail when the beaters are lifted.

6. Beat the whites with a pinch of salt until stiff but not dry.
Fold into the egg yolk mixture.

7. Shape 2 tbsps of batter into an oval and drop into the oil.
Immediately slide a metal draining spoon under the batter
to hold it in place. Place on a filled pepper. Cover the tops of
the peppers with more batter and then spoon over hot oil to
seal. Fry until the batter is brown on all sides, turning the
peppers over carefully.

8. Drain on paper towels and keep them warm on a rack in
a moderate oven while frying the remaining peppers.

9. Sprinkle with onions and serve with Red Sauce.

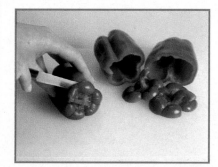

Step 2 Carefully
cut around the
stems of each
blanched pepper
to make a top.

Step 7 Cover the
tops of the peppers
with more batter
and spoon over oil
to seal.

Cook's Notes

Time
Preparation takes about 40
minutes and cooking takes
about 3 minutes per pepper. Red
Sauce will take approximately 15
minutes to cook.

Cook's Tip
Sprinkling savory foods lightly
with salt helps to draw out any
excess oil. For fried sweet foods,
substitute sugar.

Serving Ideas
Chili Rellenos may be served
as a main course with a salad
and Refried Beans. These also make a
good appetizer served with either the
Red Sauce, Green Chili Salsa or
Garden Salsa.

SERVES 4

Salad Huevos Rancheros

Chicory is becoming popular all over the United States.
This recipe puts it to delicious use with eggs and other
Tex-Mex favorites – peppers, zucchini, jicama and chorizo.

4 heads chicory
1 large red pepper, roasted (see Chicken with Red Peppers)
1 large or 2 small zucchini, cut into matchstick pieces
1 small jicama root, cut into matchstick pieces
2-3 green onions, shredded
1 chorizo sausage, blanched and cut into thin strips
4 eggs
4 tbsps pine nuts

Dressing
1 tsp chopped fresh coriander
6 tbsps oil
2 tbsps lime juice
Dash tabasco
Salt and pinch sugar

1. Prepare the roasted pepper and cut it into thin strips. Blanch the chorizo as for Indian Bread Chorizo and Salsa.

2. Separate the leaves of the chicory and slice or leave whole if small.

3. Bring water to the boil and blanch the zucchini and jicama strips for one minute. Rinse under cold water until completely cool and leave to drain. Combine with the chicory. Add the strips of chorizo and set aside.

4. Toast the pine nuts in a moderate oven until golden brown, about 5 minutes.

5. Bring at least 2 inches of water to the boil in a frying or sauté pan. Turn down the heat to simmering. Break an egg onto a saucer or into a cup.

6. Stir the water to make a whirlpool and then carefully pour the egg into the center, keeping the saucer or cup close to the level of the water. When the water stops swirling and the white begins to set, gently move the egg over to the side and repeat with each remaining egg. Cook the eggs until the whites are completely set, but the yolks are still soft.

7. Remove the eggs from the water with a draining spoon and place them immediately into a bowl of cold water.

8. Mix the dressing ingredients together and pour half over the vegetables and sausage. Toss to coat. Arrange the mixture on individual plates in the shape of nests.

9. Remove the eggs from the cold water with the draining spoon and hold them over a towel for a few minutes to drain completely. Place one egg in the middle of each nest. Spoon the remaining dressing over each egg, sprinkle over the pine nuts and garnish the yolk with a coriander leaf.

Step 6 To poach the eggs, make a whirlpool in the water and carefully pour the egg into the center.

Step 8 Arrange the vegetable mixture in the shape of a nest on a serving plate and carefully spoon an egg into the middle.

Cook's Notes

Time
Preparation takes about 45 minutes and cooking takes about 5 minutes for the eggs, 1 minute to blanch the vegetables and 10 minutes to blanch the chorizo.

Serving Ideas
Double the quantity of the vegetables and sausages and serve as a light lunch or supper dish. The salad may also be served as an appetizer.

MAKES 1 PIE

BLACK BOTTOM ICE CREAM PIE

Unbelievably simple, yet incredibly
delicious and impressive, this pie is a perfect
ending to a summer meal or a spicy one anytime.

8-10 Graham crackers, crushed
½ cup butter or margarine, melted
3 cups coffee ice cream
2oz semi-sweet chocolate, melted
4oz shredded coconut
Dark rum

1. Crush crackers with a rolling pin or in a food processor. Mix with melted butter or margarine.

2. Press into an 8½ inch false-bottomed flan dish. Chill thoroughly in the refrigerator.

3. Meanwhile, combine 4 tbsps coconut with the melted chocolate. When cooled but not solidified, add about a quarter of the coffee ice cream, mixing well.

4. Spread the mixture on the base of a crust and freeze until firm.

5. Soften the remaining ice cream with an electric mixer or food processor and spread over the chocolate-coconut layer. Re-freeze until firm.

6. Toast the remaining coconut in a moderate oven, stirring frequently until pale golden brown. Allow to cool completely.

7. Remove the pie from the freezer and leave in the refrigerator 30 minutes before serving. Push up the base of the dish and place the pie on a serving plate. Sprinkle the top with toasted coconut. Cut into wedges and drizzle with rum before serving.

Step 2 Press the crust mixture into the base and up the sides of a flan dish.

Step 4 Spread the chocolate-coconut mixture evenly over the bottom of the crust.

Step 5 Spread the coffee ice cream carefully over the chocolate-coconut layer and re-freeze.

Cook's Notes

Time
Preparation takes about 25 minutes. The ice cream will take several hours to freeze.

Freezing
The pie may be prepared well in advance and kept in the freezer for up to 3 months. Coconut may be sprinkled on top before freezing or just before serving.

Variation
If desired, use vanilla ice cream in place of the coffee.

MAKES 3 cups

GUAVA MINT SORBET

When a light dessert is called for, a
sorbet can't be surpassed. The exotic
taste of guava works well with mint.

4 ripe guavas
⅔ cup granulated sugar
1 cup water
2 tbsps chopped fresh mint
1 lime
1 egg white
Fresh mint leaves for garnish

Step 4 Process
the frozen mixture
again and
gradually work in
the egg white.

Step 2 Combine
the puréed guava,
mint and cold
syrup.

Step 3 Freeze the
mixture until slushy
and then process
to break up the ice
crystals.

1. Combine the sugar and water in a heavy-based sauce-pan and bring slowly to the boil to dissolve the sugar. When the mixture is a clear syrup, boil rapidly for 30 seconds. Allow to cool to room temperature and then chill in the refrigerator.

2. Cut the guavas in half and scoop out the pulp. Discard the peels and seeds and puree the fruit until smooth in a food processor. Add the mint and combine with cold syrup. Add lime juice until the right balance of sweetness is reached.

3. Pour the mixture into a shallow container and freeze until slushy. Process again to break up ice crystals and then freeze until firm.

4. Whip the egg white until stiff but not dry. Process the sorbet again and when smooth, add the egg white. Mix once or twice and then freeze again until firm.

5. Remove from the freezer 15 minutes before serving and keep in the refrigerator.

6. Scoop out and garnish each serving with mint leaves.

Cook's Notes

Time
Preparation takes about 2-3 hours, allowing the sorbet to freeze in between processing.

Preparation
If a food processor is not available, use an electric mixer.

Freezing
The sorbet will keep in the freezer for up to 3 months in a well-sealed, rigid container.

SERVES 6

Frozen Lime and Blueberry Cream

Blueberries grow wild in this part of the
United States and recipes to use them abound.

Juice and rind of 4 limes
Water
1 cup sugar
4oz blueberries
3 egg whites
1 cup heavy cream, whipped

Step 3 Boil the lime juice, water and sugar rapidly once a clear syrup forms.

1. Measure the lime juice and make up to 6 tbsps with water if necessary.

2. Combine with the sugar in a heavy-based pan and bring to the boil slowly to dissolve the sugar.

3. When the mixture forms a clear syrup, boil rapidly to 250°F on a sugar thermometer.

4. Meanwhile, combine the blueberries with about 4 tbsps water in a small saucepan. Bring to the boil and then simmer, covered, until very soft. Purée, sieve to remove the seeds and skin, and set aside to cool.

5. Whisk the egg whites until stiff but not dry and then pour on the hot sugar syrup in a steady stream, whisking constantly. Add the lime rind and allow the meringue to cool.

6. When cold, fold in the whipped cream. Pour in the puree and marble through the mixture with a rubber spatula. Do not over-fold. Pour the mixture into a lightly-oiled mold or bowl and freeze until firm. Leave 30 minutes in the refrigerator before serving or dip the mold for about 10 seconds in hot water. Place a plate over the bottom of the mold, invert and shake to turn out. Garnish with extra whipped cream, blueberries or lime slices.

Step 5 Pour the syrup gradually onto the whisked egg whites, beating constantly.

Step 6 Fold the cream and the fruit purée into the egg whites, marbling the purée through the mixture.

Cook's Notes

Time
Preparation takes about 40 minutes. The cream should be left in the freezer overnight to firm completely.

Variation
Substitute 2 large or 3 medium lemons for the limes. Other berries, such as raspberries, blackberries, red or black currants, may be substituted for the blueberries. If using currants, add sugar to taste.

Freezing
The cream will keep in its mold, well covered, in the freezer for up to 2 months. Remove from the freezer and leave in the refrigerator for 30 minutes or dip in hot water as the recipe suggests.

MAKES 10

FRUIT EMPANADAS

Tortillas can have a sweet side,
too, when stuffed with cheese and
sunny apricots or exotic tropical fruit.

Full quantity Tortilla recipe
10 ripe fresh apricots, halved and stoned, or 1lb canned
    apricots, well drained
1lb cream cheese
Oil for deep frying
Powdered sugar

decorative pattern.

4. Fry 1 empanada at a time until golden on both sides. Baste the upper side frequently with oil to make the tortillas puffy.

5. Drain well on paper towels and serve warm, sprinkled with powdered sugar.

Step 3 Place the cheese and apricots on the lower half of each tortilla.

Step 3 Fold over the upper half and seal the edges.

Step 3 Crimp the edges tightly into a decorative pattern.

1. Prepare the tortilla dough, roll out but do not pre-cook. Heat oil in a deep saucepan, sauté pan or deep-fat fryer to a depth of at least 2 inches. Oil should reach a temperature of 375°F.

2. Cut the apricots into quarters and the cheese into 10 even pieces.

3. Place one piece of cheese and an even amount of apricots on the lower half of each tortilla. Fold over the upper half and seal the edges. Crimp tightly into a

Cook's Notes

Time
Preparation takes about 40 minutes-1 hour for the tortillas and about 20 minutes to prepare the rest of the dish.

Variation
Other fruit may be used in the empanadas instead of apricots. Substitute fresh guava, mango or papaya cut into short strips. Sliced peaches may also be used as well as cherries, although they are not native to the Southwest.

Preparation
As with all deep-fried foods, fruit empanadas are best served as soon as they are cooked.

MAKES 1 LOAF

Chocolate Cinnamon Monkey Bread

Pull this bread apart to serve in individual pieces rather than slicing it.
Savory versions substitute Parmesan and herbs for sugar and spice.

Dough

4 tbsps warm water
1 tbsp sugar
1 envelope dry yeast
3-3¾ cups bread flour
6 tbsps sugar
Pinch salt
5 tbsps butter, softened
5 eggs

Topping

½ cup butter, melted
1 cup sugar
2 tsps cinnamon
2 tsps cocoa
6 tbsps finely chopped pecans

1. Sprinkle 1 tbsp sugar and the yeast on top of the water and leave it in a warm place until foaming.

2. Sift 3 cups of flour into a bowl and add the sugar and salt. Rub in the butter until completely blended.

3. Add 2 eggs and the yeast mixture, mixing in well. Add the remaining eggs one at a time until the mixture forms a soft, spongy dough. Add remaining flour as necessary. Knead for 10 minutes on a lightly floured surface until smooth and elastic.

4. Place the dough in a greased bowl and turn over to grease all the surfaces. Cover with plastic wrap and put in a warm place. Leave to stand for 1-1½ hours or until doubled in bulk.

5. Butter a ring mold liberally. Knock the dough down and knead it again for about 5 minutes. Shape into balls about 2 inches in diameter. Mix the topping ingredients together except for the melted butter. Roll the dough balls in the butter and then in the sugar mixture.

6. Place a layer of dough balls in the bottom of the mold and continue until all the dough and topping has been used. Cover and allow to rise again about 15 minutes. Bake in a pre-heated 350°F oven for about 45-50 minutes. Loosen from the pan and turn out while still warm.

Step 5 Roll the dough in melted butter and then in the sugar mixture.

Step 6 Lay out the balls of dough in a prepared pan.

Cook's Notes

Time
Preparation takes about 2 hours and cooking takes about 45-50 minutes.

Cook's Tip
Check the temperature of the water carefully. If it is too hot it can kill the yeast and then the bread will not rise. Water should feel warm when tested on the inside of your wrist.

Serving Ideas
Serve warm with coffee or tea, or serve as an accompaniment to a fresh fruit salad.

INDEX

Compiled by Judith Ferguson
Photographed by Peter Barry
Recipes Prepared for Photography by
Bridgeen Deery and Wendy Devenish